For Amber McManus

A Monster Surprise

小怪獸的驚喜

文 Jill McDougall

圖 余麗婷

"Look," says Purple Toes. "There is a big truck in our street."

Red Nose looks out the window. She sees a big red truck full of boxes and beds and tables.

Ma Monster looks, too. "Old Ed is *going away," she says. "He is going to another town."

"Oh no!" says Red Nose. "What about *Fluffy?"

"Fluffy is going too," says Ma.

*為生字，請參照生字表。

"That's too bad," says Purple Toes. "Fluffy plays ball with us."

"And Fluffy climbs trees with us," says Red Nose.

"And Fluffy eats our food *scraps," says Ma. "We will all miss Fluffy."

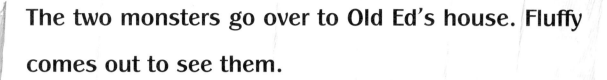

The two monsters go over to Old Ed's house. Fluffy comes out to see them.

"Hello Fluffy," says Purple Toes. "Will you miss playing ball with us?"

" *Meow," says Fluffy.

"Will you miss climbing trees with us?" says Red Nose.

"Meow, Meow," says Fluffy.

Old Ed comes out too. "Fluffy will miss eating your food scraps, too," he says. "She is getting fat."

"We will miss your fat cat," says Red Nose.

"I will send you an *email," says Old Ed. "I will send you a photo of Fluffy."

"Meow," says Fluffy.

In the morning, Red Nose gets an email from Old Ed. It says:

Hello Red Nose,

Here is a photo of Fluffy. She is still getting fat.

From

Ed

Red Nose sends an email back.

Hello Ed,

Thank you for the photo. I hope you like your new house.

From

Red Nose

The next morning, Red Nose gets a surprise.

There is another email from Old Ed. It says:

Hello Red Nose,

Fluffy has run away. I don't know where she is.

From

Ed

"Poor Ed," says Red Nose.

"Poor Fluffy," says Purple Toes.

After school, Red Nose walks past Old Ed's old house. A funny sound is coming from the *shed. She goes to the door.

"Who is there?" calls Red Nose.

The sound stops.

Red Nose opens the shed door. Something runs up to her. It is small and black.

"*Yikes!" cries Red Nose. She jumps into the air.

"Meow!" says the black thing.

"Fluffy!" *yells Red Nose. She looks inside the shed. She sees a little *nest made of *rags. Then she sees two little black faces. *Kittens! "Meow, meow," they cry.

"The kittens look just like Fluffy," says Red Nose.

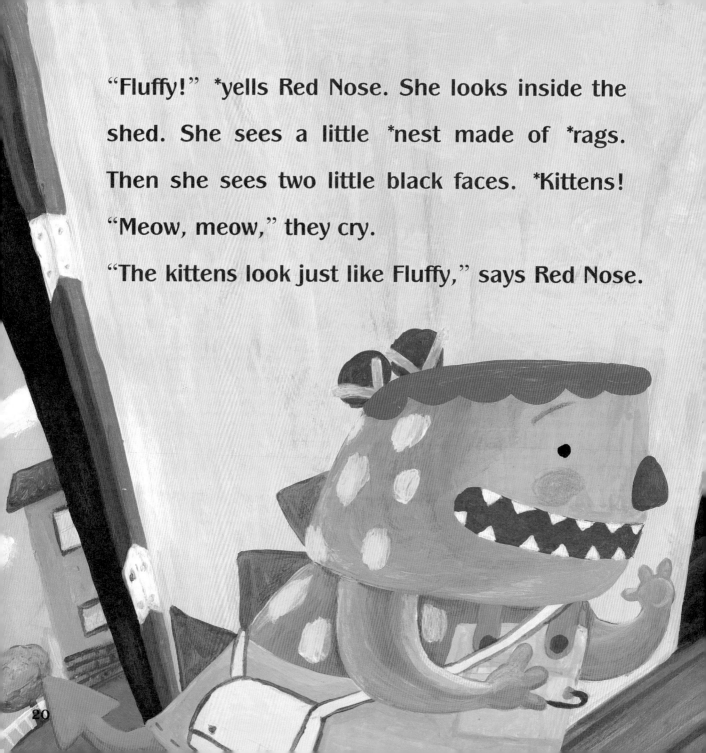

That night, Red Nose sends an email to Old Ed.

It says:

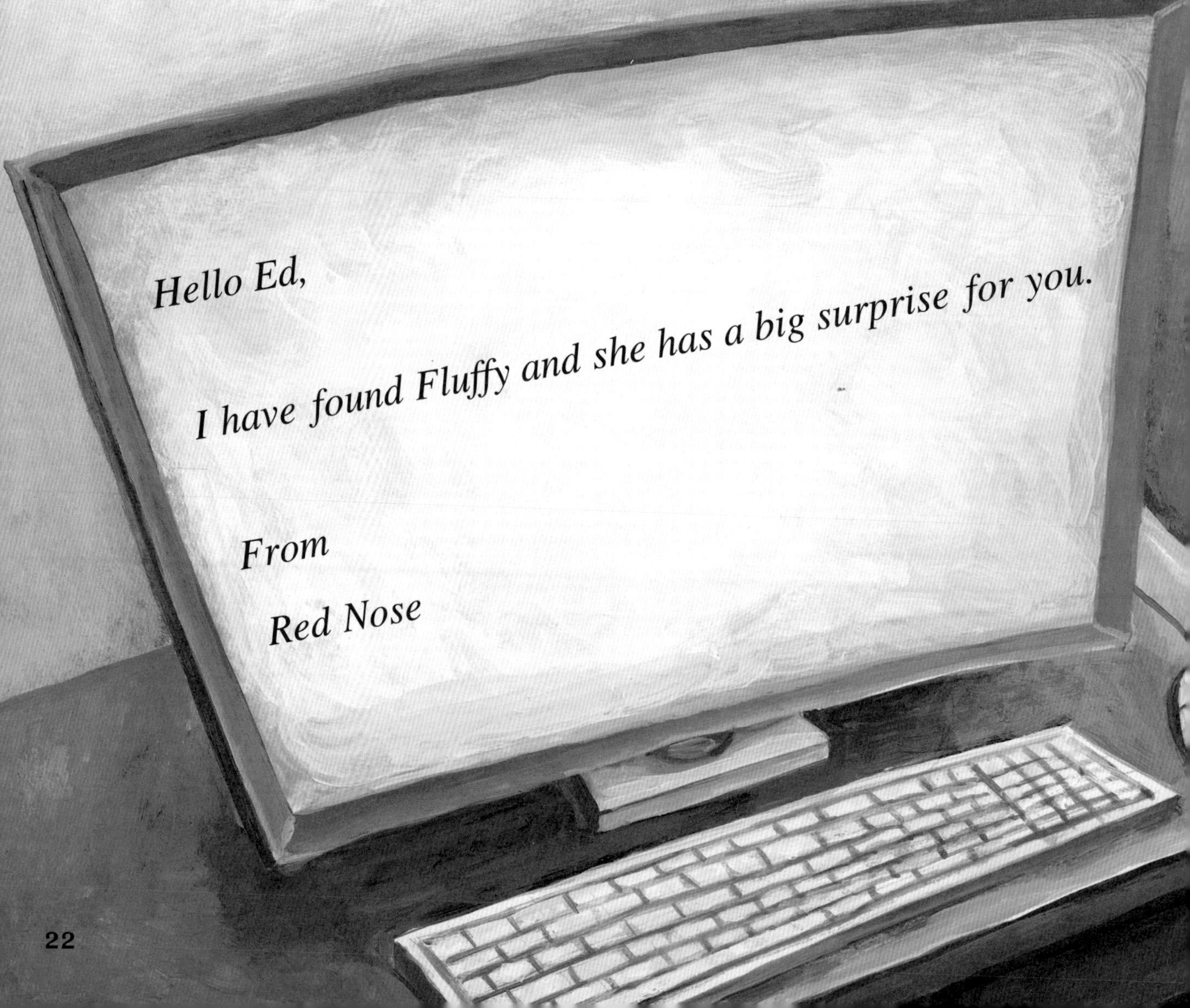

Hello Ed,

I have found Fluffy and she has a big surprise for you.

From

Red Nose

In the morning, Old Ed comes to get Fluffy. His eyes open *wide when he sees the kittens. "What a great surprise," he says.

Ma Monster gives Old Ed a box for the kittens.

"Will you keep the kittens?" she asks.

"Yes," says Old Ed. "I will keep them until they are big."

"And what then?" asks Red Nose.

"Then I must find someone to take them," says Ed.

"I must find someone to play ball with them and climb trees with them."

"And give them food scraps?" asks Red Nose.

"Yes," says Old Ed, smiling. "But not too many."

Red Nose looks at Ma. Purple Toes looks at Ma.
Ma smiles. "I know just the right place for
these kittens," she says.

31

生字表

monster [`mɑnstɚ] *n.* 怪獸

p. 4　go away　離開

fluffy [`flʌfɪ] *adj.* 蓬鬆的、毛茸茸的

（在故事中大寫當作黑貓毛毛的名字）

p. 6　scrap [skræp] *n.* 殘餘的食物

（通常用複數 scraps）

p. 8　meow [mɪ`au] *n.* 喵喵（貓的叫聲）

p. 11　email [`imel] *n.* 電子郵件

p. 16 shed [ʃɛd] *n.* 倉ㄘㄤ庫ㄎㄨ、儲ㄔㄨ藏ㄘㄤ室ㄕ

p. 18 yikes [jaɪks] *interj.* 驚ㄐㄧㄥ嚇ㄒㄧㄚ時ㄕ發ㄈㄚ出ㄔㄨ的ㄉㄜ叫ㄐㄧㄠ聲ㄕㄥ

p. 20 yell [jɛl] *v.* 大ㄉㄚ聲ㄕㄥ叫ㄐㄧㄠ喊ㄏㄢ

   nest [nɛst] *n.* 窩ㄨㄛ、巢ㄔㄠ

   rag [ræg] *n.* 碎ㄙㄨㄟ布ㄅㄨ、破ㄆㄛ布ㄅㄨ

   kitten [ˋkɪtn̩] *n.* 小ㄒㄧㄠ貓ㄇㄠ

p. 24 wide [waɪd] *adv.* 張ㄓㄤ得ㄉㄜ很ㄏㄣ大ㄉㄚ的ㄉㄜ

（詞ㄘ性ㄒㄧㄥ以ㄧ縮ㄙㄨㄛ寫ㄒㄧㄝ表ㄅㄧㄠ示ㄕ：*n.* 名ㄇㄧㄥ詞ㄘ，*adj.* 形ㄒㄧㄥ容ㄖㄨㄥ詞ㄘ，*interj.* 感ㄍㄢ嘆ㄊㄢ詞ㄘ，*v.* 動ㄉㄨㄥ詞ㄘ，*adv.* 副ㄈㄨ詞ㄘ）

小怪獸的驚喜

紫腳趾說:「妳看！有一輛大卡車停在我們的街上耶！」

紅鼻子往窗外看，看到一輛紅色的大卡車，上面裝滿了箱子、床和桌子。

怪獸媽媽也往外看，她說:「老艾德要離開這裡了，他要搬到另外一個城鎮去。」

紅鼻子說:「喔，不！那毛毛呢?」

媽媽說:「毛毛也要離開啦！」

紫腳趾說:「好可惜喔！毛毛都會和我們一起玩球。」

紅鼻子說:「而且毛毛會跟我們一起爬樹。」

媽媽說:「毛毛還會幫我們吃掉剩下來的食物。我們會很想念毛毛的。」

兩隻小怪獸走到老艾德家。毛毛跑出來看他們。

紫腳趾說:「哈囉,毛毛!妳會不會想念跟我們玩球的時候啊?」

毛毛說:「喵。」

紅鼻子說:「妳會不會想念跟我們一起爬樹的時候啊?」

毛毛說:「喵,喵。」

老艾德也走出來,他說:「毛毛也會想念你們家剩下來的食物!她越來越胖了。」

紅鼻子說:「我們會想念你的胖貓咪的。」

老艾德說:「我會寄電子郵件給你們,還會寄毛毛的照片。」

毛毛說:「喵。」

早上的時候,紅鼻子收到老艾

德寄來的電子郵件，上面寫著：

紅鼻子妳好，

這是毛毛的照片，她還是一直在變胖。

艾德上

紅鼻子回信給他：

艾德妳好，

謝謝你的照片。希望你喜歡你的新家

紅鼻子敬上

第二天早上，紅鼻子碰到一件讓她驚訝的

事。她又收到老艾德寄來的電子郵件，上

面寫著：

紅鼻子妳好，

毛毛跑掉了，我不知道她在哪裡。

艾德上

紅鼻子說：「可憐的艾德。」

紫腳趾說：「可憐的毛毛。」

放學後，紅鼻子經過老艾德的舊家時，聽到倉庫裡傳來一個奇怪的聲音。她往門那兒走去。

紅鼻子大聲說：「是誰？」

那個聲音停了下來。

紅鼻子打開倉庫的門，有個東西朝著她跑過來──它看起來又小又黑。

紅鼻子嚇得跳起來，大叫：「啊呀！」

那個黑黑的東西發出了一聲：「喵！」

紅鼻子大叫：「毛毛！」她往倉庫裡看，看到了一個用破布堆成的小窩，然後她看到兩個小小黑黑的臉。是小貓咪！

他們叫著:「喵！喵！」

紅鼻子說:「這些小貓咪長得就跟毛毛一模一樣。」

那天晚上，紅鼻子寄了一封電子郵件給老艾德，上面寫著：

艾德你好，

我已經找到毛毛了，而且她還為你準備了一個大驚喜。

紅鼻子敬上

隔天早上，老艾德來帶毛毛回去。

當他看到小貓咪的時候，眼睛張得好大好大。他說:「這真是太棒的驚喜了。」

怪獸媽媽給老艾德一個箱子裝小貓咪，然後問:「你會養這些小貓咪嗎？」

40

老艾德說:「會呀,我會一直養到他們長大一點的時候。」

紅鼻子問:「然後呢?」

艾德說:「然後我會找別人把他們帶回去養。我一定要找到可以跟他們一起玩球和爬樹的人。」

紅鼻子問:「而且會給他們剩下的食物?」

老艾德微笑著說:「沒錯,但是不能給太多。」

紅鼻子看了看媽媽。紫腳趾看了看媽媽。

媽媽笑了笑,說:「我知道哪個地方最適合這些小貓咪了。」

小怪獸教你寫電子郵件

大家好，我是紫腳趾。老艾德剛搬家的時候我有點難過，還好我們可以用電子郵件 (email) 連絡。大家對電子郵件認識有多少呢？現在就讓我為你們解釋一下吧！

當你決定好要寄信給誰後，在「收件者」欄裡填上對方的電子郵件地址 (email address)；除此之外，要在「主旨」欄裡用幾個字簡單寫下這封郵件的大意，讓對方很快瞭解你想跟他說什麼。

這裡要寫上收件人的「稱謂」，就像見面要打招呼一樣，表示尊重。

Hello Red Nose.

Here is a photo of Fluffy. She is still getting fat.

From　　　敬辭

Ed　　　你的簽名

關於郵件內容，有幾個需要注意的部份：

1. 如果是不熟的朋友，要用比較正式的稱謂稱呼對方。例如：

   Dear Mr. Monster　　親愛的怪獸先生

   Dear Miss/Mrs. Monster　　親愛的怪獸小姐／太太

   如果跟對方很熟了，就用比較輕鬆的說法：

   Dear Red Nose　　親愛的紅鼻子

   Hi Purple Toes　　嗨，紫腳趾

2. 郵件最後要寫上敬辭，並寫出自己的名字。敬辭的用法有兩種：

正式用法	非正式用法
Sincerely yours,	Best regards,
Sincerely,	Regards,
Yours truly,	Best wishes,

3. 寄出郵件前，要從頭檢查是否有寫錯字。

寫電子郵件其實不會很困難，只要大家記得一些簡單的原則，電子郵件會是一個很方便的溝通方式喔！

小怪獸教你說英文

大家好，我是紅鼻子。故事裡的毛毛 (Fluffy) 是我的好朋友，有牠陪著我，我一點都不無聊！下面是有關動物的英文，看看你對牠們了解多少！

故事裡提到貓的叫聲是「meow」，你知道其他動物的叫聲，英文要怎麼說嗎？請聽 CD 第四首的第一部分，看看他們怎麼說。

bark	（小狗）	汪汪
buzz	（蜜蜂）	嗡嗡
chirp	（小鳥）	啾啾
croak	（青蛙）	呱呱
hiss	（蛇的）	嘶嘶
quack	（鴨子）	嘎嘎
squeak	（老鼠）	吱吱

故事ㄕ裡ㄌㄧ我ㄨㄛ們ㄇㄣ叫ㄐㄧㄠ毛ㄇㄠ毛ㄇㄠ生ㄕㄥ的ㄉㄜ小ㄒㄧㄠ貓ㄇㄠ「kitten」，
那ㄋㄚ其ㄑㄧ他ㄊㄚ動ㄉㄨㄥ物ㄨ的ㄉㄜ小ㄒㄧㄠ寶ㄅㄠ寶ㄅㄠ，要ㄧㄠ怎ㄗㄣ麼ㄇㄜ用ㄩㄥ英ㄧㄥ文ㄨㄣ
表ㄅㄧㄠ達ㄉㄚ呢ㄋㄜ？請ㄑㄧㄥ聽ㄊㄧㄥ CD 第ㄉㄧ四ㄙ首ㄕㄡ的ㄉㄜ第ㄉㄧ二ㄦ部ㄅㄨ分ㄈㄣ，
跟ㄍㄣ著ㄓㄜ一ㄧ起ㄑㄧ唸ㄋㄧㄢ。

chick	小ㄒㄧㄠ雞ㄐㄧ
cub	小ㄒㄧㄠ獅ㄕ子ㄗ／小ㄒㄧㄠ老ㄌㄠ虎ㄏㄨ／小ㄒㄧㄠ熊ㄒㄩㄥ
duckling	小ㄒㄧㄠ鴨ㄧㄚ
lamb	小ㄒㄧㄠ綿ㄇㄧㄢ羊ㄧㄤ
piglet	小ㄒㄧㄠ豬ㄓㄨ
puppy	小ㄒㄧㄠ狗ㄍㄡ

作者簡介

JILL MCDOUGALL lives in a cottage by the sea in South Australia. She has been a writer ever since she could hold a pencil and has written over ninety books for children. Her stories and poems are published in countries all around the world from the USA to Sweden to South Africa. Jill is also a teacher, an animal lover and a keen organic gardener.

Jill 目前住在澳洲南部海邊的一棟小屋裡。從她學會握筆的時候，她就是一位作家了，而她寫給兒童的作品已經超過九十本。從美國到瑞典，甚至南非，都能看到她出版的詩作及故事。Jill 同時也是一位老師、動物愛好者和愛好有機作物的園藝家。

繪者簡介

余麗婷為自由插畫家，作品常見於國語日報、聯合報等，自寫自畫《家有怪物》曾獲第四屆國語日報牧笛獎。非常喜歡拍照和旅行。

她用壓克力顏料創作小怪獸系列，認為怪獸世界是充滿無限想像的。最想知道怪獸要怎麼用三隻爪子來蓋房子；最想把怪獸的爪子拿來做成餅乾造型，然後暢銷全世界。

Monster Series 小怪獸系列

學習英文0～2年者（國小1～3年級）適讀

世界上真的有怪獸嗎？
雖然他們有像恐龍一樣突起的的背脊
和尖尖的牙齒，
但是他們卻有一顆善良的心 ——
紅鼻子怪獸收留了鄰居的小貓，
紫腳趾怪獸教妹妹寫作業，
電視壞掉了，卻發現更有趣的事……

一起來探索怪獸的世界吧！

—— 小怪獸系列有三本，皆附中英雙語CD ——

1. The TV Is Mine!
   電視是我的！
2. I Hate Homework
   我討厭寫作業
3. A Monster Surprise
   小怪獸的驚喜

文／Jill McDougall
圖／余麗婷

國家圖書館出版品預行編目資料

A Monster Surprise:小怪獸的驚喜 / Jill McDougall著;
　余麗婷繪.－－初版一刷.－－臺北市：三民，2007
　　面；　公分.－－(Fun心讀雙語叢書.小怪獸系列)
中英對照
ISBN 978-957-14-4682-0　(精裝)

　1.英國語言－讀本

523.38　　　　　　　　　　　　　　　　95025209

© A Monster Surprise
—— 小怪獸的驚喜

著 作 人	Jill McDougall
繪　　者	余麗婷
責任編輯	曾鐘誼
美術設計	葉佩菱
發 行 人	劉振強
著作財產權人	三民書局股份有限公司
發 行 所	三民書局股份有限公司
	地址　臺北市復興北路386號
	電話　(02)25006600
	郵撥帳號　0009998-5
門 市 部	(復北店) 臺北市復興北路386號
	(重南店) 臺北市重慶南路一段61號
出版日期	初版一刷　2007年1月
編　　號	S 806921
定　　價	新臺幣壹佰玖拾元整

行政院新聞局登記證局版臺業字第〇二〇〇號

有著作權·不准侵害

ISBN　978-957-14-4682-0　（精裝）

http://www.sanmin.com.tw 三民網路書店
※本書如有缺頁、破損或裝訂錯誤，請寄回本公司更換。